365 EXCUSES
FOR BEING
LATE TO WORK

365 EXCUSES

FOR BEING

LATE TO WORK

ANDY SHARPE

Adams Media Corporation
HOLBROOK, MASSACHUSETTS

Published by Adams Media Corporation
260 Center Street, Holbrook, MA 02343

ISBN: 1-55850-635-7
Printed in Canada.

First Edition
J   I   H   G   F   E   D   C   B   A

Sharpe, Andy
   365 excuses for being late to work / Andy Sharpe.—1st ed.
      p.   cm.
   ISBN 1-55850-635-7
   1. Excuses—Humor. 2. Work—Humor. 3. Work
   ethic-Humor I. Title.
PN6231.E87S53 1996
818'.5402—dc20   96-21383
                                                        CIP

This book is available at quantity discounts
for bulk purchases.
For information, call 1-800-872-5627
(in Massachusetts, 617-767-8100).

Visit our home page at: http://www.adamsmedia.com

DEDICATION

To the workers of the world

ACKNOWLEDGMENTS

Thanks to my agent Nancy Stauffer and editor Pam Liflander for making my first book such a positive experience.

INTRODUCTION

Getting to work on time requires making a significant effort, and doesn't offer any tangible reward. So why bother? With all the obstacles that can cause delays, both at home and en route to work, one must plan on leaving home early each day to have any hope of consistently arriving at work on time.

This book contains a large and varied list of solid, unverifiable excuses, and explains how to best use them. In reality, most lateness is caused by a lack of effort and poor planning. However, most people need to tell their supervisors a very different story when they finally arrive at the workplace. This book contains 365 circumstances of how fate, not laziness, can intervene. It provides year-round job security for pennies a day.

Over the years I have explained my alleged plights to each of my bosses, and received responses like, "Oh, that could have happened to anyone" and "Gee, life's tough enough without having stuff like that happen." When I phone in an excuse in advance of a tardy arrival, I hear words like, "Thanks for calling, take your time, don't worry about it." This may sound like dialogue from a bad television sitcom, but it isn't. It's real!

You too can experience the joys of being late to work without getting into trouble. Just follow the six "master" rules, and use the arsenal of excuses which follows.

HOW TO USE THIS BOOK

The collection of excuses in this book is organized in two ways. The first is by time value of excuse: from three minutes to four hours. People who have a lot of self-confidence when it comes to being late choose excuses by time. When you're going to be twenty minutes late, open the book to the section of excuses rated at twenty minutes and find one you haven't used recently. This type of person won't hesitate to tell their boss that they lost a contact lens, even though they don't wear contact lenses.

The second sort is by category of excuse. This is recommended for people who only feel comfortable using excuses closely related to their own lives. People who work in the fashion industry may feel that unless their excuse falls under the category of Clothing, their supervisor will

be unsympathetic. Many people with chil-
dren have been known to get away with
being late for years using only
Parenthood excuses.

THE MASTER RULES

RULE #1. USE A GOOD EXCUSE. This book
contains 365 good excuses and is an
excellent, easy-to-use reference source.

RULE #2. VARIETY. You must vary your
excuses, the length of your latenesses,
and the days of the week on which you
are late. For some people, this means
keeping a "tardy journal." I once worked
with a guy named Mike who expected our
boss to believe that on most Mondays,
Mike's roommate's girlfriend had an
epileptic fit in his bathroom which
delayed him by forty minutes. This was a
good excuse which probably would have
worked twice a year, but Mike overused
it. One Monday, at about 9:41 A.M., our
boss had a non-epileptic fit; that was the
last time I ever saw Mike.

RULE #3. BE RESPONSIBLE. Call ahead of
time if you are going to be more than

thirty minutes late. I try to call ahead whenever I am going to use an excuse of an event that allegedly took place in my home. If I can't get to a phone, I will often change my plan of attack and use an excuse of an event that allegedly occurred after I left home.

RULE #4. LAURENCE OLIVIER IS DEAD. Do not try to be a great actor playing different roles for different excuses. Regardless of how late you are, and why, act as if you are worried that your work is going to get the best of you.

RULE #5. PLAY IT SAFE. Do not try to squeeze more mileage out of an excuse than it is worth. All the excuses in this book are conservatively time rated for your safety and convenience.

RULE #6. KNOW YOUR BOSS. Observe closely how he or she reacts when you or anyone else is late. What types of excuses are most effective? How late is too late? How often is too often?

AUTHOR'S NOTE

Consistently arriving to work more than an hour late can, over time, cause friction. Unless you are involved with something really good or really bad, you should make every effort to arrive at your job within an hour of when you are expected. Being late to work should be as simple and stress-free as stealing a pad of Post-it® Notes.

TIME

FOOD AND BEVERAGES: Refrigerator became too cold; breakfast was delayed while milk and juice thawed

SLEEP: Foot fell asleep; couldn't walk or put shoe on

CLOTHING: Slept in a pair of sweatpants with a tough knot in the drawstring; was unable to undo the knot; had to cut the drawstring to get sweatpants off

IN THE BATHROOM: Stood up too quickly after bending over to remove hair from bathtub drain; got dizzy and almost fell; needed to rest for a few minutes

4 **CAR:** Difficulty getting car out of parking space on street at home; only had three inches to spare

CITIZENSHIP: Took part in a "five-minute voter survey," which actually took much longer to complete

VETERAN: Saw a segment on the television news concerning potential health problems from eating military food

DENTAL: Sneezed while rinsing with mouthwash; bad coughing fit ensued

MALE: Tried to show a college kid going to a job interview how to tie his necktie; ended up tying it for him

FOOD AND BEVERAGES: While eating grapefruit, juice squirted into eye; irritation occurred; rinsed eye thoroughly

FINANCIAL: Fought with clerk at convenience store over whether newspaper was purchased with $10 or $20 bill

MALE: Two guys walked into each other while staring at the same woman; a fight worth watching took place

PERSONAL HEALTH: Saw the paper girl heading toward house; went outside and tried to catch her toss; missed it and ended up getting hit in the face with the newspaper

DRIVING: Hose from a home heating oil truck lay across street, blocking traffic

IN THE BATHROOM: Squeezed the baby powder container a little bit, powder shot up through the little holes; got baby powder in eyes

COMMUTING: Was listening to a morning drive radio program which became very funny; laughter became uncontrollable; for the sake of safety, pulled car over to regain composure

KEYS: Key chain broke (worth ten minutes if you are a building manager or a janitor)

CLOTHING: Sofa button caught on belt loop; had to take pants off while pinned to sofa

HOUSEPLANTS: New houseplants desperately needed sunlight; got into a wrestling match with window blinds

DRIVING: Police car driving on commuting route; all commuters were driving at speed limit and stopping when traffic signals turned yellow

FINANCIAL: ATM machine out of money

EXERCISING: Was doing deep breathing exercises; began to hyperventilate; had to lie down for a few minutes

WINTER: Was confronted by anti-fur people; needed to flee (best if wearing a fur coat)

SPIRITUAL: A man's mind plans his way, but the Lord directs his steps. (Proverbs 16:9)

HOUSEHOLD: Tried to turn off wall light switch with a drinking glass rather than a hand; glass broke

HIGH SCHOOL: Was watching a news story on TV about a former high school classmate turned criminal

POSTAL: Had to pick up a registered letter at post office—what a line!

PARENTHOOD: Noticed child had a new piercing

WILD KINGDOM: Saw a large insect at home; rather than spending the day worrying about it, pursued and captured it behind the couch; released it outdoors

PERSONAL HEALTH: Had an earring mishap (wearing a Band-Aid to hide any lack of evidence is suggested)

EYE CARE: Eyelash fell off eyelid and into eye

HOUSEHOLD: Garbage bag broke

MUSIC: Heard a great song on radio; had to know the name of the band

OTHER PEOPLE: Ran into a former good friend who is moving out of the country in three days; blah blah blah

DANGER: While at home, heard a funny noise; was concerned, but couldn't figure out where noise was coming from

PARENTHOOD: Child demanded a thorough explanation of why Australia isn't considered an island

TOTAL BLUFF: Downloaded something from the Internet, which took much longer than expected

5 MINUTES

HIGH SCHOOL: Ran into a long-winded friend from high school who comes from a large family; made the mistake of asking how her family was doing

MOM: Mom called

PERSONAL HYGIENE: A violent sneezing fit ensued after pulling out a nose hair with tweezers

FOOD AND BEVERAGES: Bagel order was screwed up twice at the coffee shop

CAR: Found homeless person sleeping in car (worth fifteen minutes if person wasn't wearing any pajamas)

FEMALE: Eyebrows were out of control

JOB-RELATED: Bumped into a coworker on the way to work; person, who shall remain nameless, started to talk about a somewhat serious, somewhat strange personal matter

CLOTHING: Static cling; unable to run for bus (train)

PARENTHOOD: Had to lecture child on responsibility

PARENTHOOD: Had to lecture child on respect

OTHER PEOPLE: Was mistaken for an elderly person's former neighbor; wanted to be polite; blah blah blah

HAIR: While showering, got strong dandruff shampoo in eye; ouch! (worth twenty minutes if contact lenses were already in)

CITIZENSHIP: Tried to give directions to visitors from another country; ran up against language barrier; ended up walking them to where they wanted to go

COMMUTING: Sat behind two people on train (bus) who were talking about new computer software; rode an extra stop; didn't really learn much

PERSONAL HEALTH: Had a problem clearing sinuses (deviated septum a plus)

WILD KINGDOM: Stepped in dog poop (worth thirty minutes if unable to clean shoe sufficiently and had to return home)

LOST AND FOUND: Found a bunch of nickels on the ground; they were too heavy and too dirty to lug to work; went to store and cashed them in for a $5 bill

KEYS: Accidentally dropped and locked keys in newspaper vending machine; not enough change to buy another paper; had to wait for another person to buy one

EX-: Phone call from ex- requesting another loan

SLEEP: Slept funny; woke up with a stiff
neck

FOOD AND BEVERAGES: Spilled a bowl of grapes, which rolled under the refrigerator and stove

SPOUSE: Spouse tried to pass decaf off as regular; showered and dressed at half-speed

DRIVING: A double-parked car, combined with a missing manhole cover, made a side street impassable

POSTAL: Stamp fell off envelope of an important letter; had to go to post office

DANGER: There was an odd smell in the house; was never able to figure out what it was

PERSONAL HEALTH: Hiccups

IN THE BATHROOM: Had major plumbing work done in bathroom yesterday; plumber inadvertently switched the hot and cold water controls

HOUSEHOLD: Freezer door wouldn't close; had ice buildup; carefully picked away ice with butter knife

IN THE BATHROOM: Slipped in the shower; more shaken up than injured

OTHER PEOPLE: Someone on train (bus) looked unhappy; asked if he wanted to talk about it; surprisingly, he did!

MUSIC: Injured shoulder playing air guitar

WILD KINGDOM: A bee flew into car during drive to work

HOUSEHOLD: Had to retrieve a salt shaker that accidentally fell into the kitchen sink disposal

VETERAN: Received a phone call about life insurance "benefits" for former members of the country's military; it took a while to realize that it was a salesperson, not a government official, on the telephone

CLOTHING: Early-morning sale; long, slow-moving check-out line; gave up; no purchase

DRIVING: Police escorting dignitary; traffic was stopped

FINANCIAL: Received long-distance phone call; can't afford to return toll calls

SPIRITUAL: Priest handed down a surprisingly stiff and time-consuming penance for two victimless sins

LOST AND FOUND: Rested wallet on something which was the same color as wallet; had a difficult time locating wallet

COMMUTING: Someone pulled emergency stop on the train for no reason

MUSIC: Had a difficult time gearing up for work because radio DJ was playing slow, depressing music

FINANCIAL: Had to find an old canceled check because of a bookkeeping error made by a large company

MALE: Left the toilet seat up; realized it en route to work; returned home

14 **TOTAL BLUFF:** Accidentally swallowed an ice cube while drinking a breakfast beverage; had difficulty speaking and breathing until ice cube melted enough to slide into stomach

10 MINUTES

IN THE BATHROOM: Took a shower; realized that all the towels were in the wash; dried off with paper towels and a pillowcase

FOOD AND BEVERAGES: Slow-moving drive-thru line at the fast food restaurant

POSTAL: Cut tongue on envelope while licking it; rinsed mouth with warm salt water

MUSIC: Was one of ten lucky call-in winners of a radio station music trivia contest; had to stay on phone to claim prize

HOUSEHOLD: Vacuum cleaner sucked up fringe of rug; had a very difficult time prying the rug loose

DEAF: Was eavesdropping on a conversation by lip reading; found out about a bank robbery scheme; had to go to the police immediately

EYE CARE: Forgot reading glasses; returned home (do you have reading glasses?)

HAIR: Got hair spray in eyes

PARENTHOOD: Child couldn't find security blanket; day care drop-off was delayed until blanket was found

DRIVING: Encountered funeral procession; traffic was stopped

WINTER: Forgot to refill humidifiers before leaving for work; returned home

EXERCISING: Morning jog took much longer than usual because of sore muscles

16 **WILD KINGDOM:** Discovered an ant invasion at home; called upon Mr. Vacuum Cleaner

CAR: Had a problem with automatic garage door

FINANCIAL: Received a phone call offering seventy-five tax-free dollars to switch long-distance companies

HIGH SCHOOL: Ran into a former classmate who had a sex change operation

OTHER PEOPLE: A department store mistakenly tried to deliver a new refrigerator; delivery driver needed to use telephone

FOOD AND BEVERAGES: Timer malfunctioned on coffeemaker at home

MALE: Neck was badly irritated from shaving; had to apply face cream and warm water

SPIRITUAL: Religious service lasted longer than usual

PARENTHOOD: Lost a lot of time taking deep breaths and counting slowly to ten

EX-: Phone call from ex- wanting to "voice new concerns"

KEYS: Keys fell behind stove; ended up having to use a coat hanger and a flashlight to retrieve them

IN THE BATHROOM: Light bulb failed in complicated single-bulb bathroom light/fan fixture; had difficulty replacing bulb

FINANCIAL: Bank called to report unusual activity on credit card; discovered card had been stolen!

SLEEP: Sleep was interrupted three times by wrong-number phone calls; overslept

PERSONAL HEALTH: Injured toe running barefoot for ringing telephone

SPIRITUAL: A man's steps are ordered by the Lord; how then can man understand his way? (Proverbs 20:24)

VETERAN: Received an important phone call regarding participation in this year's Veterans Day Parade

CLOTHING: Early-morning wash of needed work clothes fell behind schedule when the unattended washing machine stopped because load became "unbalanced"

COMMUTING: Didn't realize that a new bus (train) schedule went into effect this week

SPOUSE: Was confronted with the "we need to talk" line

PERSONAL HEALTH: Had a splinter

SLEEP: Had a very romantic dream involving someone famous; didn't want to wake up

MALE: Left for work wearing a bow tie; chickened out; returned home to change

CLOTHING: On way to work, stepped on and broke an untied shoelace; went to the cobbler and was given a free used replacement shoelace by the nice man

HOUSEHOLD: Blew two fuses (circuit breaker tripped twice) using new microwave oven

DENTAL: Dental floss frayed and got stuck between teeth

OTHER PEOPLE: A needy family member (roommate) had the need to talk; couldn't shake the person

JOB-RELATED: Remembered boss's ailment just before leaving for work; consulted alternative medicine books looking for remedy; recommendation: take Vitamin C

CITIZENSHIP: Went to make a clothing donation to a homeless shelter before work; discovered the drop-off site had moved (this excuse is better if you drive to work)

MOM: Needed to call Mom and wish her a good trip before she left; phone line was busy; Mom doesn't believe in call waiting

LOST AND FOUND: Couldn't find eyeglasses; no one around to help in the search (it's difficult to find stuff when you can't see!)

20 **TOTAL BLUFF:** Engine was knocking badly from cheap gasoline; had to stop and buy high-octane gasoline

15 MINUTES

SPIRITUAL: Was chanting for better relationship with boss; lost track of time

CLOTHING: Shrunken underwear was very uncomfortable; returned home for a bigger pair

IN THE BATHROOM: Noticed dandruff after showering; had to wash and dry hair again

PARENTHOOD: Child forgot to bring lunch to school; delivered it before heading to work (an ideal excuse if you have a child with dietary restrictions)

SPOUSE: Noticed spouse wasn't planning on wearing wedding ring to work; had a heated discussion

WILD KINGDOM: Wild dogs were roaming the neighborhood; couldn't safely get into car until dogs went to terrorize someone else

CLOTHING: Laundry was stolen from dryer at laundromat; had no underwear; had to buy a pair on way to work

WINTER: Turned heat way up to take chill out of home; forgot to turn it down before leaving for work; returned home

VETERAN: Dry cleaner lost a button off of military uniform; had a difficult time convincing store owner it will cost $40 to replace

MOM: Forgot Mom's birthday; made emergency phone calls to Mom and florist

CITIZENSHIP: Witnessed the theft of a police car

OTHER PEOPLE: A very pregnant friend who can no longer fit behind a steering wheel needed a ride

FINANCIAL: A movie was being shot in my neighborhood; was offered $30 to tie shoe on the fender of a new Mercedes Benz; had to do five takes

OTHER PEOPLE: Received a three-way conference call from family members regarding holiday plans

FOOD AND BEVERAGES: Drove over a loaf of bread, but thought it was an animal; doubled back to investigate

HIGH SCHOOL: Ran into the mother of an old high school friend; blah blah blah

EYE CARE: Couldn't see well; realized both contact lenses were in the same eye; returned home

COMMUTING: Bus was too crowded; couldn't board; had to wait for next one

COMMUTING: Bus, which is always crowded, was totally empty; became suspicious and decided to wait for next one

HOUSEHOLD: Melted a plastic container in microwave oven

LOST AND FOUND: Found a wallet on way to work; brought it to police station; had to fill out many forms

FEMALE: Was startled by a loud noise when applying mascara; the mascara brush and some mascara ended up in eye; ouch!

MALE: Left for work with the beginnings of a mustache and/or long sideburns; chickened out; returned home and shaved (best on first day of work week)

DRIVING: Drawbridge was up (worth 50 minutes if it malfunctioned)

IN THE BATHROOM: Drain clogged; couldn't leave home; crystal drain cleaner had to be flushed after fifteen minutes

EXERCISING: Weight machine at gym broke; got trapped under weights

PERSONAL HEALTH: Very itchy feet; returned home to change socks; guessing new inexpensive brand of laundry detergent is to blame

DEAF: Was reading an interesting editorial in newspaper; didn't feel train come into the station

EYE CARE: While combing hair, accidentally poked self in eye

SPIRITUAL: Aggravated old knee injury while praying before leaving for work

MALE: Left home with a noticeably missed shaving spot; stopped to buy a cheap razor

STAR TREKKING: Up very late watching a disappointing meteor shower; overslept (not to be used by people employed at astronomy labs)

HOUSEPLANTS: Tried to move a thriving houseplant to a larger flowerpot; couldn't get plant to stand upright in its new home

CAR: After stopping to buy a newspaper, returned to car; found a double-parked delivery truck blocking it in

WILD KINGDOM: Drove over a small animal; pulled car over and cried

EX-: All movements were controlled by ex- using a voodoo doll

PARENTHOOD: Nipple of child's pacifier missing; needed to find it to be sure it wasn't swallowed

FINANCIAL: Winning lottery numbers dream; had to stay asleep until all the numbers were drawn

FOOD AND BEVERAGES: Badly burnt toast; smoke detector went crazy

DRIVING: Traffic signals out of synch with each other; semi-gridlock situation ensued, with only one or two cars making it through each light cycle

HAIR: Tried a new hairstyle that required a lot of gel; it didn't work out; had to wash hair again

PERSONAL HYGIENE: Cotton from discount-brand cotton swab fell off in ear; had to retrieve it with tweezers

FEMALE: Got distracted by a phone call while bleaching mustache; checked in the mirror before leaving for work and realized that only one side of mustache had been bleached

HOUSEHOLD: Vacuumed up a rare button that fell off an old coat; had to sift through bag to retrieve it

SLEEP: Slept funny; woke up with a deep pillow line on face; steamed it out

TOTAL BLUFF: Was returning three rented videos; happened to notice none were rewound; had to return home to avoid fines

20 MINUTES

SPOUSE: Spouse is on a sequestered jury; conjugal visit ran later than expected

COMMUTING: Commuter smelled; got off bus rather than cause hurt feelings by switching seats

WINTER: Water vapor from humidifier damaged alarm clock; clock stopped

PERSONAL HEALTH: Upset stomach; went to small ethnic convenience store in neighborhood for stomach medicine; brought medicine home; realized instructions were in foreign language; went back to store for a translation

MALE: While shaving, accidentally dropped razor in toilet; went to store to replace it

FEMALE: Left for work wearing too much perfume; returned home; showered

PARENTHOOD: Child removed and hid shoelaces from all adult shoes

DRIVING: Was ten cents short for the automated exact-change toll booth; too many vehicles in line to back up; was trapped; drove through without paying; was stopped by police officer

EYE CARE: Accidentally fell asleep with contact lenses in; they became stuck to eyes

HOUSEPLANTS: Was watering hanging houseplants; muddy water dripped down onto an expensive piece of stereo equipment which needed to be taken apart and cleaned immediately

FOOD AND BEVERAGES: Drank an ice-cold glass of juice too quickly; got a very painful "frozen brain" headache

CLOTHING: Pulled on a loose thread during commute; a hole developed; returned home to change

HIGH SCHOOL: On way to work, ran into high school teacher who was a major influence; what a guy!

SLEEP: Didn't sleep well; dogs in neighborhood were barking at sirens and then at each other much of the night

JOB-RELATED: Stopped to buy a box of donuts for coworkers (don't forget donuts!)

CITIZENSHIP: Registered to vote; City Hall was disorganized

SPIRITUAL: Dropped statue of chubby spiritual leader on foot

EYE CARE: Left home wearing colored contact lenses; chickened out; returned home

IN THE BATHROOM: Killed a fly on bathroom mirror; unfortunately mirror broke

DRIVING: Traffic reporter on radio suggested alternate route; primary route was "a mess"

FINANCIAL: ATM machine didn't release amount of money requested; argued with service representative on ATM phone

WILD KINGDOM: Left home with a lot of dog (cat) hair on clothes; returned home to use special animal hair remover brush

MUSIC: Left stereo turntable on; remembered it en route to work; returned home

SPIRITUAL: Church bells in neighborhood rang at the wrong time

OTHER PEOPLE: Was following a friend who was bringing car to a mechanic to be repaired; lost fast-driving friend

PARENTHOOD: Accidentally tipped over child's biology experiment growing in the refrigerator; had to wait for child to leave for school before trying to put it back together

COMMUTING: Train (bus) came and went ahead of schedule

STAR TREKKING: Valued model of original Enterprise displayed on sunny windowsill melted; carefully molded ship back into shape while plastic was malleable

EX-: Was winning a heated phone discussion with ex-; didn't want to end conversation

CLOTHING: Noticed on way to work that today's outfit looked a lot like yesterday's outfit; returned home

KEYS: Couldn't find keys when ready to depart for work; had left them overnight in lock on outside of front door

FOOD AND BEVERAGES: On way to work, remembered carton of milk had been left on kitchen counter; returned home

HOUSEHOLD: Wasn't feeling well; took body temperature; dropped and broke thermometer; had great difficulty picking up mercury

FINANCIAL: Attempted to do banking by phone

CAR: Was stopped by police; another person's car was stolen; wrong Lojack™ was activated

PERSONAL HYGIENE: Had a difficult time washing off a large, conspicuous temporary tattoo

OTHER PEOPLE: Saw someone on train (bus) who needed to be avoided; got off, took next one

PERSONAL HEALTH: Water got into inner ear during shower

MOM: Forgot to set VCR to record Mom's favorite TV program; returned home

LOST AND FOUND: On way to work, found a decent chair in someone's curbside garbage; brought it home

HOUSEHOLD: Floor wax didn't dry overnight; had to climb out of a window to avoid stepping on sticky floors

TOTAL BLUFF: Daub a lot of calamine lotion on face; no one will even ask . . .

FINANCIAL: A weather situation affecting soybean crop developed overnight; needed to hedge an aggressive futures position by doing some trading in both national and foreign markets

CLOTHING: Encountered long line at convenience store; clothes became unwearable because of secondhand smoke; returned home

DRIVING: Banged on dashboard hoping to stop mysterious rattle; driver's side air bag accidentally opened

HOUSEHOLD: Street at home being dug up with jackhammers; vibrations caused framed painting to fall off the wall; had to sweep up glass and store painting properly

LOST AND FOUND: Screw fell out of hinge of eyeglasses; replaced it on the way to work

REPRODUCTION: Forgot to take birth control pill; returned home

FINANCIAL: Bank called; a deposited check bounced; cash needed to be dropped off at a branch office immediately to cover checks to two utility companies

PERSONAL HYGIENE: Toenail scissors got stuck on thumb; had to use ice and cooking oil to remove them

OTHER PEOPLE: A friend with a job interview needed to use shower and hair dryer

HOUSEHOLD: Defrosted refrigerator overnight; found kitchen floor flooded in the morning

PARENTHOOD: Child took a long shower with shower curtain outside bathtub

CAR: Noticed that someone had placed a racist bumper sticker on car; removed it with a kitchen knife, vinegar, and a sponge

WINTER: Someone drove into a fire hydrant; water turned into ice; couldn't get up hill on street

PERSONAL HEALTH: Got carried away giving breast self-examination

PERSONAL HEALTH: Got carried away giving testicular self-examination

DANGER: Carbon monoxide detector went off; had to call and wait for the natural gas company

CLOTHING: Had too much sticky stuff on soles of shoes following previous night's trip to movie theater; trash on sidewalks kept getting stuck to shoes; couldn't stand it; returned home to change shoes

FEMALE: Noticed a funny discharge; read reference book, called doctor

DRIVING: Left home without driver's license (best for pizza and package delivery people)

FOOD AND BEVERAGES: Ate at a restaurant before heading for work; forgot to leave a tip; realized this en route to work; returned to restaurant

LOST AND FOUND: Earring fell off; returned to where hat (sweater) was removed; found it!

IN THE BATHROOM: Fell asleep taking a bath

HOUSEPLANTS: Discovered houseplant had been invaded by some sort of bug; changed the soil and washed the plant with warm salty water

OTHER PEOPLE: When driving to work, saw black-sheep cousin hitchhiking; gave him a ride to the bus station after stopping at the bank to lend him money until "he gets settled"

WILD KINGDOM: A bird's wing got stuck in feeder hanging on tree; had to climb up on a ladder to free the bird

COMMUTING: Was listening to two people on bus (train) having a very boring conversation; fell asleep; missed stop

JOB-RELATED: Took day's worth of smoking breaks at beginning of work day

WILD KINGDOM: Bug bites on feet were itching like crazy; returned home to wash feet and change socks

SPOUSE: Was cutting onions and began to cry; spouse was unaware of the onion cutting and felt guilty about recent lack of quality time; apologies, hugs, kisses, etc.

CITIZENSHIP: Was out late celebrating cultural diversity

MALE: Accidentally wore a white T-shirt with a beer logo printed on it underneath dress shirt; noticed while adjusting necktie en route to work; returned home to change

EYE CARE: Contact lens dissolved during enzyme cleaning; stopped and got a replacement on way to work

FOOD AND BEVERAGES: Accidentally sat on a full container of yogurt; had to change clothes and clean off couch

CAR: Tried to re-register car; needed to pay an old parking ticket at City Hall first

KEYS: Had trouble with key to new burglar alarm system

PARENTHOOD: Diaper delivery service was late; had to go to store for disposables

SPIRITUAL: Therapist fell asleep; didn't notice, kept talking; appointment ran late

TOTAL BLUFF: A valuable Oriental rug fell out of a truck onto road; stopped to move rug; realized what it was; waited hoping truck wouldn't return; unfortunately, truck did eventually return

STAR TREKKING: Got to work on time; forgot to turn off cloaking device

SLEEP: Took a nighttime pain reliever with sleep aid for the first time; wow!

CLOTHING: Discovered moths in sweater drawer

CAR: After getting in car, noticed oil hadn't been changed in 5,500 miles; went straight to the garage

EYE CARE: Accidentally put contact lens cleaner, rather than eye drops, in eye; very painful!

EXERCISING: No hot water at the gym; needed to return home to shower

DEAF: Alarm clock's wake-up light was working when alarm first went off; however, it burnt out after hitting the doze button; didn't wake up until a large truck drove by home

FOOD AND BEVERAGES: Had leftover Chinese food for breakfast; had a bad reaction to the MSG

DANGER: Got gasoline on clothing at self-serve gas station; returned home

SPIRITUAL: Psychiatrist planted a false memory that today was a holiday

MUSIC: Heard a great symphony on radio; needed to find out composer and opus number

OTHER PEOPLE: DJ on radio announced the wrong time

FOOD AND BEVERAGES: Early-morning trip to the grocery store; clerk forgot to put expensive item into shopping bag; discovered mistake at home; returned to store

PARENTHOOD: Tried in vain to get chewing gum off an expensive rug

COMMUTING: Bus driver new to bus route made a very wrong turn

HOUSEPLANTS: Forgot to water vacationing neighbor's plants three days ago; suddenly remembered en route to work; went directly to neighbor's home

PERSONAL HEALTH: Sneezed violently, causing inner ear to go crazy

FEMALE: Menstrual situation

FEMALE: Premenstrual situation

CITIZENSHIP: Threw away refrigerator; had difficult time getting doors off (child safety issue)

EYE CARE: Contact lens got stuck way up in eye; difficult to find; difficult to retrieve

HAIR: Left home with shampoo in hair

PARENTHOOD: A new bully situation has developed; had to drive child to school

WILD KINGDOM: Pet food crisis: electric can opener motor burnt out while trying to open can of pet food; had to go to store for dry pet food

JOB-RELATED: Job interview lasted longer than expected (proceed with caution with this one)

CAR: Bought gasoline on way to work; gas station attendant failed to put gas cap back on; had to return to the gas station

REPRODUCTION: Took a home pregnancy test; got an ambiguous result; waited; then took test again

DRIVING: School bus broke down; no one could pass it—state law

CLOTHING: Realized shoes didn't match; returned home

OTHER PEOPLE: A drunk neighbor drove his car into a light pole, knocking out electricity and telephone service in neighborhood; overslept; no hot water and no phone

PERSONAL HEALTH: Overdid it experimenting with the medicinal benefits of garlic

WILD KINGDOM: Small animal crawled into the engine area of car; it wasn't pretty

FINANCIAL: Participated in an overnight medical study; testing ran late

WINTER: Parked car against snow bank; tail pipe clogged with snow and ice; had to go to the convenience store to buy a cigarette lighter to induce melting

CITIZENSHIP: Gave blood before work; got dizzy; had to rest

IN THE BATHROOM: Had some trouble with the toilet

TOTAL BLUFF: Got angry at the misinformation on a television newscast; threw a shoe at the TV, shattering the picture tube

50 MINUTES

EXERCISING: Couldn't get out of a yoga position

PARENTHOOD: Child had a temper tantrum; objects broken, keys hidden

WINTER: Slipped on ice and lost balance; didn't fall, but seam in pants split; returned home

IN THE BATHROOM: No cold water for shower; had to take a bath; cooled tub with ice cubes and refrigerated spring water

OTHER PEOPLE: Did a favor for a friend; please don't ask . . .

HOUSEHOLD: A dish towel was accidentally left in the dishwasher, causing a very bad overflow situation

MALE: Noticed cotton pants had shrunk and were much too short; returned home to change

KEYS: Friend lost her keys; I'm the keeper of the extra set

CLOTHING: While waiting for bus (train), leaned against a freshly painted streetlight pole

FINANCIAL: ATM card no longer readable; went to bank for money and to apply for a new card

CAR: Dropped off car to be repaired; promised loaner car unavailable

REPRODUCTION: Ovulating

REPRODUCTION: Wife was ovulating

REPRODUCTION: Neighbor's wife was ovulating

COMMUTING: Had a flat tire

WILD KINGDOM: Pet gerbil crawled into a small dark hole; had a difficult time retrieving it

PERSONAL HEALTH: Lifted box at home; forgot to bend from the knees; did some stretching and applied ice to lower back

CITIZENSHIP: Spotted profane graffiti on the sidewalk near an elementary school; went to hardware store to buy spray paint; returned to graffiti site and changed it to a hockey word

DANGER: Had home tested for radon; the radon tester had a problem calibrating equipment

FEMALE: Realized breasts not secured with brassiere; returned home

FOOD AND BEVERAGES: Dropped a quart of milk when taking it out of refrigerator; most of it ended up under refrigerator

CAR: Ran out of gas; discovered gas gauge was broken; it no longer reads below 1/4 of a tank

SLEEP: Couldn't sleep:had dinner previous evening at a restaurant where waitress accidentally served regular coffee rather than decaf

TOTAL BLUFF: A sheet of water from window washers fell from the sky; clothing was soaked; returned home to change

60 MINUTES

CAR: Power went out at drive-thru car wash; car got caught in between brushes

EYE CARE: Mistakenly put in roommate's contact lenses; couldn't see well; returned home

DENTAL: Forgot to put in bridgework;
returned home

PERSONAL HEALTH: Pollen and/or mold
spores caused flare-up of allergies; had to
wait for medication to kick in

COMMUTING: Hit a big pothole (driving,
biking); vehicle needed to be dropped off
for repair

FEMALE: Drove with part of dress sticking
out of car door; dress became soiled;
returned home to change (wet roads a plus)

WINTER: Car doors were frozen shut (had
been to the car wash the previous evening)

WILD KINGDOM: Pet lost a fight; it had
to be taken to the vet

POSTAL: Accidentally dropped address
book in mailbox while mailing letters

CLOTHING: Couldn't squeeze into any clean
pants (skirt); went to one-hour dry cleaner

DANGER: Downed power lines in front of
home

HOUSEHOLD: Pilot light went out in gas oven; kitchen filled with natural gas

EXERCISING: Work clothes stolen from locker room at gym; returned home

FEMALE: Had an allergic reaction to a different brand of mascara

PARENTHOOD: Discovered a lot of money in child's room; confronted child; would rather not say any more

TOTAL BLUFF: Found a Catholic bishop's outfit on the ground in front of home; searched for and eventually found an open Catholic church

70 MINUTES

FEMALE: Acidentally put on slip instead of dress; returned home to change

PERSONAL HEALTH: Had migraine headache (you have to get them to understand)

CLOTHING: Three people on bus (train) pointed out that clothes didn't match; returned home

SPOUSE: Switched cars for the day with spouse; spouse left home first;didn't have key to spouse's antitheft device

FINANCIAL: IRS showed up unexpectedly to see possessions—it's part of the audit process

PARENTHOOD: Outbreak of mumps at day care center; had to make other arrangements

COMMUTING: Left something on train (bus); waited for it to circle back on its route

OTHER PEOPLE: Neighbor went into labor; had to watch neighbor's kid until grandmother arrived

STAR TREKKING: Abducted by aliens during the night; was returned to wrong address

TOTAL BLUFF: Was drinking herbal tea; accidentally swallowed the tea bag; went to the emergency room where a doctor said nothing needed to be done, but suggested drinking lots of water for the next twenty-four hours

80 MINUTES

HAIR: During shower, water company turned off water; shampoo was still in hair; had to go to store and buy bottled water to rinse hair

FOOD AND BEVERAGES: Put kettle on for coffee; forgot about it; left; remembered it; returned home; kettle ruined

WILD KINGDOM: Cat (dog) swallowed a collar bell; pet had to be taken to the vet

CAR: Car windshield was cracked during the night by a bird feeder that fell out of the tree next to the driveway

CLOTHING: Pen in shirt pocket leaked badly; returned home to shower and change clothing

OTHER PEOPLE: Received a phone call when leaving for work from black-sheep cousin who needed $250 to get out of jail on bail; would rather not discuss the charges

PERSONAL HYGIENE: Girlfriend (boyfriend) took last pair of clean underwear; had to do a wash

TOTAL BLUFF: Was going to call in sick but am feeling a little better; will be coming in late

EYE CARE: Broke eyeglasses; was able to get identical pair; what luck!

CAR: Got an oil change; car lift malfunctioned; couldn't get car down

WINTER: Wooden front door at home contracted from the cold and dryness of winter air, causing the gap between the door and frame to grow; front door lock was too far from door frame; needed to have locksmith replace lock bolt with a longer one

COMMUTING: While biking to work, pants caught between bicycle derailleur and chain; pants were ruined; returned home to change

HAIR: Tried to lighten hair a little bit at home; ended up with a white patch of hair on back of head; sought aid from a hair care professional

WILD KINGDOM: Was scratched and possibly bitten by a stray dog; rabies scare; went to doctor

TOTAL BLUFF: A private matter; would rather not say any more

SLEEP: Slept on a docked houseboat that broke its moorings and drifted out to sea

WILD KINGDOM: Insect flew into ear; went to doctor

KEYS: Locked keys in car; called AAA; they didn't rush over

CAR: Possible defect in braking system; car recalled by auto maker

PARENTHOOD: Child in trouble at school; had an emergency parent/faculty conference

TOTAL BLUFF: Was watching a television show on hypnotism; accidentally got hypnotized; snapped out of it when a neighbor's dog started barking

240 MINUTES

MOM: Mom's house flooded; went there to help out

EXERCISING: Had a bad reaction to chlorine in pool at the gym

CITIZENSHIP: Stopped for making an illegal U-turn; was arrested and jailed overnight because a person with outstanding arrest warrants has same name and date of birth

DENTAL: Was eating an "all-natural" breakfast cereal; broke a filling when biting into a small stone; needed emergency dental care

FOOD AND BEVERAGES: Food poisoning from sushi/egg salad

TOTAL BLUFF: What do you mean, late?; I was given the day off; only came in to use the bathroom; I'll stay if you need me to

CATEGORY

CAR

3 MINUTES: Difficulty getting car out of parking space on street at home; only had three inches to spare

5 MINUTES: Found homeless person sleeping in car (worth fifteen minutes if person wasn't wearing any pajamas)

10 MINUTES: Had a problem with automatic garage door

15 MINUTES: After stopping to buy a newspaper, returned to car; found a double-parked delivery truck blocking it in

20 MINUTES: Was stopped by police; another person's car was stolen; wrong Lojack™ was activated

30 MINUTES: Noticed that someone had placed a racist bumper sticker on car; removed it with a kitchen knife, vinegar, and a sponge

30 MINUTES: Tried to re-register car; needed to pay an old parking ticket at City Hall first

40 MINUTES: After getting in car, noticed oil hadn't been changed in 5,500 miles; went straight to the garage

40 MINUTES: Bought gasoline on way to work; gas station attendant failed to put gas cap back on; had to return to the gas station

50 MINUTES: Ran out of gas; discovered gas gauge was broken; it no longer reads below 1/4 of a tank

50 MINUTES: Dropped off car to be repaired; promised loaner car was unavailable

60 MINUTES: Power went out at drive-thru car wash; car got caught in between brushes

80 MINUTES: Car windshield was cracked during the night by a bird feeder that fell out of the tree next to the driveway

90 MINUTES: Got an oil change; car lift malfunctioned; couldn't get car down

120 MINUTES: Possible defect in braking system; car recalled by auto maker

CITIZENSHIP

3 MINUTES: Took part in a "five-minute voter survey," which actually took much longer to complete

5 MINUTES: Tried to give directions to visitors from another country; ran up against language barrier; ended up walking them to where they wanted to go

10 MINUTES: Went to make a clothing donation to a homeless shelter before work; discovered the drop-off site had moved (this excuse is better if you drive to work)

15 MINUTES: Witnessed the theft of a police car

20 MINUTES: Registered to vote; City Hall was disorganized

30 MINUTES: Was out late celebrating cultural diversity

40 MINUTES: Gave blood before work; got dizzy; had to rest

40 MINUTES: Threw away refrigerator; had difficult time getting doors off (child safety issue)

50 MINUTES: Spotted profane graffiti on the sidewalk near an elementary school; went to hardware store to buy spray paint; returned to graffiti site and changed it to a hockey word

240 MINUTES: Stopped for making an illegal U-turn; was arrested and jailed overnight because a person with outstanding arrest warrants has same name and date of birth

CLOTHING

3 MINUTES: Sofa button caught on belt loop; had to take pants off while pinned to sofa

3 MINUTES: Slept in a pair of sweatpants with a tough knot in the drawstring; was unable to undo the knot; had to cut the drawstring to get sweatpants off

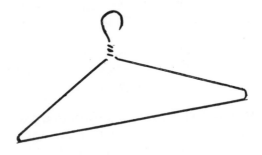

5 MINUTES: Early-morning sale; long, slow-moving check-out line; gave up; no purchase

5 MINUTES: Static cling; unable to run for bus (train)

10 MINUTES: Early-morning wash of needed work clothes fell behind schedule when the unattended washing machine stopped because load became "unbalanced"

10 MINUTES: On way to work, stepped on and broke an untied shoelace; went to the cobbler and was given a free used replacement shoelace by the nice man

15 MINUTES: Shrunken underwear was very uncomfortable; returned home for a bigger pair

15 MINUTES: Laundry was stolen from dryer at laundromat; had no underwear; had to buy a pair on way to work

20 MINUTES: Noticed on way to work that today's outfit looked a lot like yesterday's outfit; returned home to change

20 MINUTES: Pulled on a loose thread during commute; a hole developed; returned home to change

30 MINUTES: Encountered long line at convenience store; clothes became unwearable because of secondhand smoke; returned home

30 MINUTES: Had too much sticky stuff on soles of shoes following previous night's trip to movie theater; trash on sidewalks kept getting stuck to shoes; couldn't stand it; returned home to change shoes

40 MINUTES: Realized shoes didn't match; returned home

40 MINUTES: Discovered moths in sweater drawer

50 MINUTES: While waiting for bus (train), leaned against a freshly painted streetlight pole

60 MINUTES: Couldn't squeeze into any clean pants (skirt); went to one-hour dry cleaner

70 MINUTES: Three people on bus (train) pointed out that clothes didn't match; returned home to change

80 MINUTES: Pen in shirt pocket leaked badly; returned home to shower and change clothing

COMMUTING

3 MINUTES: Was listening to a morning drive radio program which became very funny; laughter became uncontrollable; for the sake of safety, pulled car over to regain composure

5 MINUTES: Sat behind two people on train (bus) who were talking about new computer software; rode an extra stop; didn't really learn much

5 MINUTES: Someone pulled emergency stop on the train for no reason

10 MINUTES: Didn't realize that a new bus (train) schedule went into effect this week

15 MINUTES: Bus was too crowded; couldn't board; had to wait for next one

15 MINUTES: Bus, which is always crowded, was totally empty; became suspicious and decided to wait for next one

20 MINUTES: Commuter smelled; got off bus rather than cause hurt feelings by switching seats

20 MINUTES: Train (bus) came and went ahead of schedule

30 MINUTES: Was listening to two people on bus (train) having a very boring conversation; fell asleep; missed stop

40 MINUTES: Bus driver new to bus route made a very wrong turn

50 MINUTES: Had a flat tire

60 MINUTES: Hit a big pothole (driving, biking); vehicle needed to be dropped off for repair

70 MINUTES: Left something on train (bus); waited for it to circle back on its route

90 MINUTES: While biking to work, pants caught between bicycle derailleur and chain; pants were ruined; returned home to change

DANGER

3 MINUTES: While at home, heard a funny noise; was concerned, but couldn't figure out where noise was coming from

5 MINUTES: There was an odd smell in the house; wasn't able to figure out what it was

30 MINUTES: Carbon monoxide detector went off; had to call and wait for the natural gas company

40 MINUTES: Got gasoline on clothing at self-serve gas station; returned home to change

50 MINUTES: Had home tested for radon; the radon tester had a problem calibrating equipment

60 MINUTES: Downed power lines in front of home

DEAF

10 MINUTES: Was eavesdropping on a conversation by lip-reading; found out about a bank robbery scheme; had to go to the police immediately

15 MINUTES: Was reading an interesting editorial in newspaper; didn't feel train come into the station

40 MINUTES: Alarm clock's wake-up light was working when alarm first went off; however, it burnt out after hitting the doze button; didn't wake up until a large truck drove by home

DENTAL

3 MINUTES: Sneezed while rinsing with mouthwash; bad coughing fit ensued

10 MINUTES: Dental floss frayed and got stuck between teeth

60 MINUTES: Forgot to put in bridge-work; returned home

240 MINUTES: Was eating an "all-natural" breakfast cereal; broke a filling when
biting into a small stone; needed emergency dental care

DRIVING

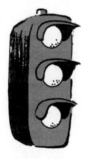

3 MINUTES: Hose from a home heating oil
truck lay across street, blocking traffic

3 MINUTES: Police car driving on commuting route; all commuters were driving at speed limit and stopping when
traffic signals turned yellow

5 MINUTES: Police escorting dignitary;
traffic was stopped

5 MINUTES: A double-parked car, combined with a missing manhole cover, made a side street impassable

10 MINUTES: Encountered funeral procession; traffic was stopped

15 MINUTES: Drawbridge was up (worth 50 minutes if it malfunctioned)

15 MINUTES: Traffic signals out of synch with each other; semi-gridlock situation ensued, with only one or two cars making it through each light cycle

20 MINUTES: Traffic reporter on radio suggested alternate route; primary route was "a mess"

20 MINUTES: Was ten cents short for the automated exact-change toll booth; too many vehicles in line to back up; was trapped; drove through without paying; was stopped by police officer

30 MINUTES: Left home without driver's license (best for pizza and package delivery people)

30 MINUTES: Banged on dashboard hoping to stop a mysterious rattle; driver's side air bag accidentally opened

40 MINUTES: School bus broke down; no one could pass it—state law

EX-

5 MINUTES: Phone call from ex- requesting another loan

10 MINUTES: Phone call from ex- wanting to "voice new concerns"

15 MINUTES: All movements were controlled by ex- using a voodoo doll

20 MINUTES: Was winning a heated
phone discussion with ex-; didn't want to
end conversation

EXERCISING

3 MINUTES: Was doing deep breathing
exercises; began to hyperventilate; had to
lie down for a few minutes

10 MINUTES: Morning jog took much
longer than usual because of sore muscles

15 MINUTES: Weight machine at gym
broke; got trapped under weights

40 MINUTES: No hot water at the gym;
needed to return home to shower

50 MINUTES: Couldn't get out of a yoga position

60 MINUTES: Work clothes stolen from locker room at gym; returned home

240 MINUTES: Had a bad reaction to chlorine in pool at the gym

EYE CARE

3 MINUTES: Eyelash fell off eyelid and into eye

10 MINUTES: Forgot reading glasses; returned home (do you have reading glasses?)

15 MINUTES: While combing hair, accidentally poked self in eye

15 MINUTES: Couldn't see well; realized both contact lenses were in the same eye; returned home

20 MINUTES: Accidentally fell asleep with contact lenses in; they became stuck to eyes

20 MINUTES: Left home wearing colored contact lenses; chickened out; returned home

30 MINUTES: Contact lens dissolved during enzyme cleaning; stopped and got a replacement on way to work

40 MINUTES: Contact lens got stuck way up in eye; difficult to find; difficult to retrieve

40 MINUTES: Accidentally put contact lens cleaner, rather than eye drops, in eye; very painful!

60 MINUTES: Mistakenly put in roommate's contact lenses; couldn't see well; returned home

90 MINUTES: Broke eyeglasses; was able to get identical pair; what luck!

FEMALE

5 MINUTES: Eyebrows were out of control

15 MINUTES: Was startled by a loud noise when applying mascara; the mascara brush and some mascara ended up in eye; ouch!

15 MINUTES: Got distracted by a phone call while bleaching mustache; checked in the mirror before leaving for work and realized that only one side of mustache had been bleached

20 MINUTES: Left for work wearing too much perfume; returned home; showered

30 MINUTES: Noticed a funny discharge; read reference book, called doctor

40 MINUTES: Menstrual situation

40 MINUTES: Premenstrual situation

50 MINUTES: Realized breasts not secured with brassiere; returned home

60 MINUTES: Drove with part of dress sticking out of car door; dress became soiled; returned home to change (wet roads a plus)

60 MINUTES: Had an allergic reaction to a different brand of mascara

70 MINUTES: Accidentally put on slip instead of dress; returned home to change

FINANCIAL

3 MINUTES: ATM machine out of money

3 MINUTES: Fought with clerk at convenience store over whether newspaper was purchased with $10 or $20 bill

5 MINUTES: Received long-distance phone call; can't afford to return toll calls

5 MINUTES: Had to find an old canceled check because of a bookkeeping error made by a large company

10 MINUTES: Bank called to report unusual activity on credit card; discovered card had been stolen!

10 MINUTES: Received a phone call offering seventy-five tax-free dollars to switch long distance companies

15 MINUTES: Winning lottery numbers dream; had to stay asleep until all the numbers were drawn

15 MINUTES: A movie was being shot in my neighborhood; was offered $30 to tie shoe on the fender of a new Mercedes Benz; had to do five takes

20 MINUTES: ATM machine didn't release amount of money requested; argued with service representative on ATM phone

20 MINUTES: Attempted to do banking by phone

30 MINUTES: A weather situation affecting soybean crop developed overnight; needed to hedge an aggressive futures position by doing some trading in both national and foreign markets

30 MINUTES: Bank called; a deposited check bounced; cash needed to be dropped off at a branch office immediately to cover checks to two utility companies

40 MINUTES: Participated in an overnight medical study; testing ran late

50 MINUTES: ATM card no longer readable; went to bank for money and to apply for a new card

70 MINUTES: IRS showed up unexpectedly to see possessions—it's part of the audit process

FOOD AND BEVERAGES

3 MINUTES: While eating grapefruit, juice squirted into eye; irritation occurred; rinsed eye thoroughly

3 MINUTES: Refrigerator became too cold; breakfast was delayed while milk and juice thawed

5 MINUTES: Bagel order was screwed up twice at the coffee shop

5 MINUTES: Spilled a bowl of grapes, which rolled under the refrigerator and stove

10 MINUTES: Slow-moving drive-thru line at the fast food restaurant

10 MINUTES: Timer malfunctioned on coffeemaker at home

15 MINUTES: Badly burnt toast; smoke detector went crazy

15 MINUTES: Drove over a loaf of bread, but thought it was an animal; doubled back to investigate

20 MINUTES: On way to work, remembered carton of milk had been left on kitchen counter; returned home

20 MINUTES: Drank an ice-cold glass of juice too quickly; got a very painful "frozen brain" headache

30 MINUTES: Ate at a restaurant before heading for work; forgot to leave a tip; realized this en route to work; returned to restaurant

30 MINUTES: Accidentally sat on a full container of yogurt; had to change clothes and clean off couch

40 MINUTES: Had leftover Chinese food for breakfast; had a bad reaction to the MSG

40 MINUTES: Early-morning trip to the grocery store; clerk forgot to put expensive item into shopping bag; discovered mistake at home; returned to store

50 MINUTES: Dropped a quart of milk when taking it out of refrigerator; most of it ended up under refrigerator

80 MINUTES: Put kettle on for coffee; forgot about it; left; remembered it; returned home; kettle ruined

240 MINUTES: Food poisoning from sushi/egg salad

HAIR

5 MINUTES: While showering, got strong dandruff shampoo in eye; ouch! (worth twenty minutes if contact lenses were already in)

10 MINUTES: Got hair spray in eyes

15 MINUTES: Tried a new hairstyle that required a lot of gel; it didn't work out; had to wash hair again

40 MINUTES: Left home with shampoo in hair

80 MINUTES: During shower, water company turned off water; shampoo was still in hair; had to go to store and buy bottled water to rinse hair

90 MINUTES: Tried to lighten hair a little bit at home; ended up with a white patch of hair on back of head; sought aid from a hair care professional

HIGH SCHOOL

3 MINUTES: Was watching a news story on TV about a former high school classmate turned criminal

5 MINUTES: Ran into a long-winded friend from high school who comes from a large family; made the mistake of asking how her family was doing

10 MINUTES: Ran into a former classmate who had a sex change operation

15 MINUTES: Ran into the mother of an old high school friend; blah blah blah

20 MINUTES: On way to work, ran into high school teacher who was a major influence; what a guy!

HOUSEHOLD

3 MINUTES: Tried to turn off wall light switch with a drinking glass rather than a hand; glass broke

3 MINUTES: Garbage bag broke

5 MINUTES: Freezer door wouldn't close; had ice buildup; carefully picked away ice with butter knife

5 MINUTES: Had to retrieve a salt shaker that accidentally fell into the kitchen sink disposal

10 MINUTES: Vacuum cleaner sucked up fringe of rug; had a very difficult time prying the rug loose

10 MINUTES: Blew two fuses (circuit breaker tripped twice) using new microwave oven

15 MINUTES: Vacuumed up a rare button that fell off an old coat; had to sift through bag to retrieve it

15 MINUTES: Melted a plastic container in microwave oven

20 MINUTES: Wasn't feeling well; took body temperature; dropped and broke thermometer; had great difficulty picking up mercury

20 MINUTES: Floor wax didn't dry overnight; had to climb out of a window to avoid stepping on sticky floors

30 MINUTES: Street at home being dug up with jackhammers; vibrations caused a framed painting to fall off the wall; had to sweep up glass and store painting properly

30 MINUTES: Defrosted refrigerator overnight; found kitchen floor flooded in the morning

50 MINUTES: A dish towel was accidentally left in the dishwasher, causing a very bad overflow situation

60 MINUTES: Pilot light went out in gas oven; kitchen filled with natural gas

HOUSEPLANTS

3 MINUTES: New houseplants desperately needed sunlight; got into a wrestling match with window blinds

15 MINUTES: Tried to move a thriving houseplant to a larger flowerpot; couldn't get plant to stand upright in its new home

20 MINUTES: Was watering hanging houseplants; muddy water dripped down onto an expensive piece of stereo equipment which needed to be taken apart and cleaned immediately

30 MINUTES: Discovered houseplant had been invaded by some sort of bug; changed the soil and washed the plant with warm salty water

40 MINUTES: Forgot to water vacationing neighbor's plants three days ago; suddenly remembered en route to work; went directly to neighbor's home

IN THE BATHROOM

3 MINUTES: Squeezed the baby powder container a little bit, powder shot up through the little holes; got baby powder in eyes

3 MINUTES: Stood up too quickly after bending over to remove hair from bathtub drain; got dizzy and almost fell; needed to rest for a few minutes

5 MINUTES: Had major plumbing work done in bathroom yesterday; plumber inadvertently switched the hot and cold water controls

5 MINUTES: Slipped in the shower; more shaken up than injured

10 MINUTES: Light bulb failed in complicated single-bulb bathroom light/fan fixture; had difficulty replacing bulb

10 MINUTES: Took a shower; realized that all the towels were in the wash; dried off with paper towels and a pillowcase

15 MINUTES: Drain clogged; couldn't leave home; crystal drain cleaner had to be flushed after fifteen minutes

15 MINUTES: Noticed dandruff after showering; had to wash and dry hair again

20 MINUTES: Killed a fly on bathroom mirror; unfortunately mirror broke

30 MINUTES: Fell asleep taking a bath

40 MINUTES: Had some trouble with the toilet

50 MINUTES: No cold water for shower; had to take a bath; cooled tub with ice cubes and refrigerated spring water

JOB-RELATED

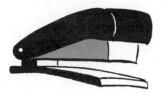

5 MINUTES: Bumped into a coworker on the way to work; person, who shall remain nameless, started to talk about a somewhat serious, somewhat strange personal matter

10 MINUTES: Remembered boss's ailment just before leaving for work; consulted alternative medicine books looking for remedy; recommendation: take Vitamin C

20 MINUTES: Stopped to buy a box of donuts for coworkers (don't forget donuts!)

30 MINUTES: Took day's worth of smoking breaks at beginning of work day

40 MINUTES: Job interview lasted longer than expected (proceed with caution with this one)

KEYS

3 MINUTES: Key chain broke (worth ten minutes if you are a building manager or a janitor)

5 MINUTES: Accidentally dropped and locked keys in newspaper vending machine; not enough change to buy another paper; had to wait for another person to buy one

10 MINUTES: Keys fell behind stove; ended up having to use a coat hanger and a flashlight to retrieve them

20 MINUTES: Couldn't find keys when ready to depart for work; had left them overnight in lock on outside of front door

30 MINUTES: Had trouble with key to new burglar alarm system

50 MINUTES: Friend lost her keys; I'm the keeper of the extra set

120 MINUTES: Locked keys in car; called AAA; they didn't rush over

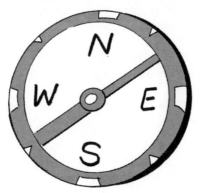

5 MINUTES: Found a bunch of nickels on the ground; they were too heavy and too dirty to lug to work; went to store and cashed them in for a $5 bill

5 MINUTES: Rested wallet on something which was the same color as wallet; had a difficult time locating wallet

10 MINUTES: Couldn't find eyeglasses; no one around to help in the search (it's difficult to find stuff when you can't see!)

15 MINUTES: Found a wallet on way to work; brought it to police station; had to fill out many forms

20 MINUTES: On way to work, found a decent chair in someone's curbside garbage; brought it home

30 MINUTES: Screw fell out of hinge of eyeglasses; replaced it on the way to work

30 MINUTES: Earring fell off; returned to where hat (sweater) was removed; found it!

MALE

3 MINUTES: Tried to show a college kid going to a job interview how to tie his necktie; ended up tying it for him

3 MINUTES: Two guys walked into each other while staring at the same woman; a fight worth watching took place

5 MINUTES: Left the toilet seat up; realized it en route to work; returned home

10 MINUTES: Left for work wearing a
bow tie; chickened out; returned home to
change

10 MINUTES: Neck was badly irritated
from shaving; had to apply face cream
and warm water

15 MINUTES: Left home with a noticeably
missed shaving spot; stopped to buy a
cheap razor

15 MINUTES: Left for work with the
beginnings of a mustache and/or long
sideburns; chickened out; returned home
and shaved (best on first day of work
week)

20 MINUTES: While shaving, accidentally
dropped razor in toilet; went to store to
replace it

30 MINUTES: Accidentally wore a white
T-shirt with a beer logo printed on it
underneath dress shirt; noticed while
adjusting necktie en route to work;
returned home to change

50 MINUTES: Noticed cotton pants had shrunk and were much too short; returned home to change

MOM

5 MINUTES: Mom called

10 MINUTES: Needed to call Mom and wish her a good trip before she left; phone line was busy; Mom doesn't believe in call-waiting

15 MINUTES: Forgot Mom's birthday: emergency phone calls to Mom and florist

20 MINUTES: Forgot to set VCR to record
Mom's favorite TV program; returned
home

240 MINUTES: Mom's house flooded;
went there to help out

MUSIC

3 MINUTES: Heard a great song on radio;
had to know the name of the band

5 MINUTES: Had a difficult time gearing
up for work; radio DJ was playing slow,
depressing music

5 MINUTES: Injured shoulder playing air
guitar

10 MINUTES: Was one of ten lucky call-in winners of a radio station music trivia contest; had to stay on phone to claim prize

20 MINUTES: Left stereo turntable on; remembered it en route to work; returned home

40 MINUTES: Heard a great symphony on radio; needed to find out composer and opus number

OTHER PEOPLE

3 MINUTES: Ran into a former good friend who is moving out of the country in three days; blah blah blah

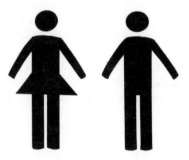

5 MINUTES: Someone on train (bus) looked unhappy; asked if he wanted to talk about it; surprisingly, he did!

5 MINUTES: Was mistaken for an elderly person's former neighbor; wanted to be polite; blah blah blah

10 MINUTES: A needy family member (roommate) had the need to talk; couldn't shake free

10 MINUTES: A department store mistakenly tried to deliver a new refrigerator; delivery driver needed to use telephone

15 MINUTES: Received a three-way conference call from family members regarding holiday plans

15 MINUTES: A very pregnant friend who can no longer fit behind a steering wheel needed a ride

20 MINUTES: Saw someone on train (bus) who needed to be avoided; got off, took next one

20 MINUTES: Was following a friend who was bringing car to a mechanic to be repaired; lost fast-driving friend

30 MINUTES: A friend with a job interview needed to use shower and hair dryer

30 MINUTES: When driving to work, saw black-sheep cousin hitchhiking; gave him a ride to the bus station after stopping at the bank to lend him money until "he gets settled"

40 MINUTES: DJ on radio announced the wrong time

40 MINUTES: A drunk neighbor drove his car into a light pole, knocking out electricity and telephone service in neighborhood; overslept; had no hot water and no phone

50 MINUTES: Did a favor for a friend; please don't ask . . .

70 MINUTES: Neighbor went into labor; had to watch neighbor's kid until grandmother arrived

80 MINUTES: Received a phone call when leaving for work from black-sheep cousin who needed $250 to get out of jail on bail; would rather not discuss the charges

PARENTHOOD

3 MINUTES: Noticed child had a new piercing

3 MINUTES: Child demanded a thorough explanation of why Australia isn't considered an island

5 MINUTES: Had to lecture child on responsibility

5 MINUTES: Had to lecture child on respect

10 MINUTES: Lost a lot of time taking deep breaths and counting slowly to ten

10 MINUTES: Child couldn't find security blanket; day care drop-off was delayed until blanket was found

15 MINUTES: Child forgot to bring lunch to school; delivered it before heading to work (an ideal excuse if you have a child with dietary restrictions)

15 MINUTES: Nipple of child's pacifier missing; needed to find it to be sure it wasn't swallowed

20 MINUTES: Accidentally tipped over child's biology experiment growing in the refrigerator; had to wait for child to leave for school before trying to put it back together

20 MINUTES: Child removed and hid shoelaces from all adult shoes

30 MINUTES: Diaper delivery service was late; had to go to store for disposables

30 MINUTES: Child took a long shower with shower curtain outside bathtub

40 MINUTES: A new bully situation has developed; had to drive child to school

40 MINUTES: Tried in vain to get chewing gum off an expensive rug

50 MINUTES: Child had a temper tantrum; objects broken, keys hidden

60 MINUTES: Discovered a lot of money in child's room; confronted child; would rather not say any more

70 MINUTES: Outbreak of mumps at day care center; had to make other arrangements

120 MINUTES: Child in trouble at school; had an emergency parent/faculty conference

PERSONAL HEALTH

3 MINUTES: Had an earring mishap (wearing a Band-Aid to hide any lack of evidence is suggested)

3 MINUTES: Saw the paper girl heading toward house; went outside and tried to catch her toss; missed it and ended up getting hit in the face with the newspaper

5 MINUTES: Hiccups

5 MINUTES: Had a problem clearing sinuses (deviated septum a plus)

10 MINUTES: A splinter

10 MINUTES: Injured toe running barefoot for ringing telephone

15 MINUTES: Very itchy feet; returned home to change socks; guessing new inexpensive brand of laundry detergent is to blame

20 MINUTES: Water got into inner ear during shower

20 MINUTES: Upset stomach; went to small ethnic convenience store in neighborhood for stomach medicine; brought medicine home; realized instructions were in foreign language; went back to store for a translation

30 MINUTES: Got carried away giving breast self-examination

30 MINUTES: Got carried away giving testicular self-examination

40 MINUTES: Overdid it experimenting with the medicinal benefits of garlic

40 MINUTES: Sneezed violently, causing inner ear to go crazy

50 MINUTES: Lifted box at home; forgot to bend from the knees; did some stretching and applied ice to lower back

60 MINUTES: Pollen and/or mold spores caused flare-up of allergies; had to wait for medication to kick in

70 MINUTES: Had migraine headache
(you have to get them to understand)

PERSONAL HYGIENE

5 MINUTES: A violent sneezing fit ensued
after pulling out a nose hair with tweezers

15 MINUTES: Cotton from discount-brand
cotton swab fell off in ear; had to retrieve
it with tweezers

20 MINUTES: Had a difficult time washing off a large, conspicuous temporary
tattoo

30 MINUTES: Toenail scissors got stuck
on thumb; had to use ice and cooking oil
to remove them

80 MINUTES: Girlfriend (boyfriend) took last pair of clean underwear; had to do a wash

POSTAL

3 MINUTES: Had to pick up a registered letter at post office—what a line!

5 MINUTES: Stamp fell off envelope of an important letter; had to go to post office

10 MINUTES: Cut tongue on envelope while licking it; rinsed mouth with warm salt water

60 MINUTES: Accidentally dropped address book in mailbox while mailing letters

REPRODUCTION

30 MINUTES: Forgot to take birth control pill; returned home

40 MINUTES: Took a home pregnancy test; got an ambiguous result; drank a lot of water; waited; then took test again

50 MINUTES: Ovulating

50 MINUTES: Wife was ovulating

50 MINUTES: Neighbor's wife was ovulating

SLEEP

3 MINUTES: Foot fell asleep; couldn't walk or put shoe on

5 MINUTES: Slept funny; woke up with a stiff neck

10 MINUTES: Had a very romantic dream involving someone famous; didn't want to wake up

10 MINUTES: Sleep was interrupted three times by wrong-number phone calls; overslept

15 MINUTES: Slept funny; woke up with a deep pillow line on face; steamed it out

20 MINUTES: Didn't sleep well; dogs in neighborhood were barking at sirens and then at each other much of the night

40 MINUTES: Took a nighttime pain reliever with sleep aid for the first time; wow!

50 MINUTES: Couldn't sleep: had dinner previous evening at a restaurant where waitress accidentally served regular coffee rather than decaf

120 MINUTES: Slept on a docked houseboat that broke its moorings and drifted out to sea

SPIRITUAL

3 MINUTES: A man's mind plans his way, but the Lord directs his steps. (Proverbs 16:9)

5 MINUTES: Priest handed down a surprisingly stiff and time-consuming penance for two victimless sins

10 MINUTES: Religious service lasted longer than usual

10 MINUTES: A man's steps are ordered by the Lord; how then can man understand his way? (Proverbs 20:24)

15 MINUTES: Was chanting for better relationship with boss; lost track of time

15 MINUTES: Aggravated old knee injury while praying before leaving for work

20 MINUTES: Dropped statue of chubby spiritual leader on foot

20 MINUTES: Church bells in neighborhood rang at the wrong time

30 MINUTES: Therapist fell asleep; didn't notice, kept talking; appointment ran late

40 MINUTES: Psychiatrist planted a false memory that today was a holiday

SPOUSE

5 MINUTES: Spouse tried to pass decaf off as regular; showered and dressed at half-speed

10 MINUTES: Was confronted with the "we need to talk" line

15 MINUTES: Noticed spouse wasn't planning on wearing wedding ring to work; had a heated discussion

20 MINUTES: Spouse is on a sequestered jury; conjugal visit ran later than expected

30 MINUTES: Was cutting onions and began to cry; spouse was unaware of the onion cutting and felt guilty about recent lack of quality time; apologies, hugs, kisses, etc.

70 MINUTES: Switched cars for the day with spouse; spouse left home first; didn't have key to spouse's antitheft device

STAR TREKKING

15 MINUTES: Up very late watching a disappointing meteor shower; overslept (not to be used by people employed at astronomy labs)

20 MINUTES: Valued model of original Enterprise displayed on in sunny windowsill melted; carefully molded ship back into shape while plastic was malleable

40 MINUTES: Got to work on time; forgot to turn off cloaking device

70 MINUTES: Abducted by aliens during the night; was returned to wrong address

TOTAL BLUFF

3 MINUTES: Downloaded something from the Internet, which took much longer than expected

5 MINUTES: Accidentally swallowed an ice cube while drinking a breakfast beverage; had difficulty speaking and breathing until ice cube melted enough to slide into stomach

10 MINUTES: Engine was knocking badly from cheap gasoline; had to stop and buy high-octane gasoline

15 MINUTES: Was returning three rented videos; happened to notice none were rewound; had to return home to avoid fines

20 MINUTES: Daub a lot of calamine lotion on face; no one will even ask . . .

30 MINUTES: A valuable Oriental rug fell out of a truck onto road; stopped to move rug; realized what it was; waited hoping truck wouldn't return; unfortunately, truck did eventually return

40 MINUTES: Got angry at the misinformation on a television newscast; threw a shoe at the TV, shattering the picture tube

50 MINUTES: A sheet of water from window washers fell from the sky; clothing was soaked; returned home to change

60 MINUTES: Found a Catholic bishop's outfit on the ground in front of home; searched for and eventually found an open Catholic church

70 MINUTES: Was drinking herbal tea; accidentally swallowed the tea bag; went to the emergency room, where a doctor said nothing needed to be done, but suggested drinking lots of water for the next twenty-four hours

80 MINUTES: Was going to call in sick but am feeling a little better; will be coming in late

90 MINUTES: A private matter; would rather not say any more

120 MINUTES: Was watching a television show on hypnotism; accidentally got hypnotized; snapped out of it when a neighbor's dog started barking

240 MINUTES: What do you mean, late? I was given the day off; only came in to use the bathroom; I'll stay if you need me to

VETERAN

3 MINUTES: Saw a segment on the television news concerning potential health problems from eating military food

5 MINUTES: Received a phone call about life insurance "benefits" for former members of the country's military; it took a while to realize that it was a salesperson, not a government official, on the telephone

10 MINUTES: Received an important phone call regarding participation in this year's Veterans Day Parade

15 MINUTES: Dry cleaner lost a button off of military uniform; had a difficult time convincing store owner it will cost $40 to replace

WILD KINGDOM

3 MINUTES: Saw a large insect at home; rather than spending the day worrying about it, pursued and captured it behind the couch; released it outdoors

5 MINUTES: A bee flew into car while driving to work

5 MINUTES: Stepped in dog poop (worth thirty minutes if unable to clean shoe sufficiently and had to return home)

10 MINUTES: Discovered an ant invasion at home; called upon Mr. Vacuum Cleaner

15 MINUTES: Drove over a small animal; pulled car over and cried

15 MINUTES: Wild dogs were roaming the neighborhood; couldn't safely get into car until dogs went to terrorize someone else

20 MINUTES: Left home with a lot of dog (cat) hair on clothes; returned home to use special animal hair remover brush

30 MINUTES: A bird's wing got stuck in feeder hanging on tree; had to climb up on a ladder to free the bird

30 MINUTES: Bug bites on feet were itching like crazy; returned home to wash feet and change socks

40 MINUTES: Small animal crawled into the engine area of car; it wasn't pretty

40 MINUTES: Pet food crisis: electric can opener motor burnt out while trying to open can of pet food; had to go to store for dry pet food

50 MINUTES: Pet gerbil crawled into a small dark hole; had a difficult time retrieving it

60 MINUTES: Pet lost a fight; it had to be taken to the vet

80 MINUTES: Cat (dog) swallowed a collar bell; pet had to be taken to the vet

90 MINUTES: Was scratched and possibly bitten by a stray dog; rabies scare; went to doctor

120 MINUTES: Insect flew into ear; went to doctor

3 MINUTES: Was confronted by anti-fur people; needed to flee (best if wearing a fur coat)

10 MINUTES: Forgot to refill humidifiers before leaving for work; returned home

15 MINUTES: Turned heat way up to take chill out of home; forgot to turn it down before leaving for work; returned home

20 MINUTES: Water vapor from humidifier damaged alarm clock; clock stopped

30 MINUTES: Someone drove into a fire hydrant; water turned into ice; couldn't get up hill on street

40 MINUTES: Parked car against snow bank; tail pipe clogged with snow and ice; had to go to the convenience store to buy a cigarette lighter to induce melting

50 MINUTES: Slipped on ice and lost balance; didn't fall, but seam in pants split; returned home

60 MINUTES: Car doors were frozen shut (had been to the car wash the previous evening)

90 MINUTES: Wooden front door at home contracted from the cold and dryness of winter air, causing the gap between the door and frame to grow; front door lock was too far from door frame; needed to have locksmith replace lock bolt with a longer one